THE TEENS GUIDE TO BECOMING AN ENTREPRENEUR

102 Ways That You Can Start to Think
Like a Successful Entrepreneur.

Tanya Rogers
David Rogers

Rogers Publishing

Selling For Kids Book Series
Volume 1 - The Kids Guide To Selling: How I was Able To Make $4,000 in 60 Days
Volume 2 - The Teens Guide To Starting Your Own Business: Your Step by Step Blueprint to Becoming a Teen Entrepreneur
Volume 3 - The Teens Guide to Becoming an Entrepreneur: 102 Ways That You Can Start to Think Like a Successful Entrepreneur.

We can not guarantee that your results will be the same as the author's. This material is for educational purposes only.

Cover design by: David Rogers
Printed in the United States of America

CONTENTS

FREE EBOOK

We Want You To Get The Most From The Selling For Kids Book Series

Get your FREE Bonus eBook from Selling for Kids. This is an exclusive offer for Readers of The Selling for Kids Series. It's currently not available on Amazon and only available from the link below.

SellingForKids.com/BONUS

INTRODUCTION

Welcome to Selling for Kids Volume 3, *The Teens Guide to Becoming an Entrepreneur: 102 Ways That You Can Start to Think Like a Successful Entrepreneur*. We started The Selling for Kids Book Series to teach a future generation of young entrepreneurs what it takes to succeed.

In our first book, *The Kids Guide to Selling,* we teach you about the nine fundamental principles you need to know to start your first business. Plus, you learn what you need to do Right Now to start selling and generating an income, following our simple and inexpensive business model.

In our second book, *The Teens Guide to Starting Your Own Business,* we dig even deeper into the concepts of starting your own business and becoming a teen entrepreneur. Plus, we give you the step-by-step Blueprint of what, when, and how you need to do to launch your first business successfully.

In this book, *The Teens Guide to Becoming an Entrepreneur: 102 Ways That You Can Start to Think Like a Successful Entrepreneur*. We will take that knowledge to the next level by introducing you to the idea of creating the Entrepreneur's Mindset. We will be showing you 102 ways that you can start to think like a successful entrepreneur.

This book will be your roadmap of what you need to learn to become successful. It is for anyone who wants to learn how to be successful in life, and you don't need to read the first two books in the series to understand what we are going to be talking about here.

Of course, we hope you have already read the first two books. If you have, then hopefully, you have already started the business model we teach and made your first $4,000 or more. You can keep doing that business model as long as you like. We just want you to be prepared to take the next step of your entrepreneurial career. You can take all the money you earned in your first business and then use it to open your next successful business.

CHAPTER 1: WHY YOU SHOULD BECOME AN ENTREPRENEUR?

"As long as you are alive, you will either live to accomplish your own goals and dreams or be used as a resource to accomplish someone else's."

- GRANT CARDONE

A recent survey found that more than 60% of people want to become entrepreneurs or start their own business. Becoming an entrepreneur is an in-demand job or career choice for many reasons, including pride, purpose, and sometimes money. Starting and then running your own business on a day-to-day basis is not an easy task, but it is worth the effort.

Why Should You Consider Becoming An Entrepreneur?

There are thousands of reasons why you should take that giant step and create your own business.

Here are just a few of them:

Autonomy – The idea of running your own business allows you to be in charge of your destiny. It can help you to avoid getting stuck in the "daily grind," or as Rich Dad Poor Dad's author Robert Kiyosaki puts it, the "rat race." For many entrepreneurs, running their own business lets them have a self-sustaining career.

Opportunity – By becoming an entrepreneur, you will open up a whole new world of opportunity for you. You will have the chance to do anything that you want in life. Being an entrepreneur gives you the ability to either create real change in the world or to live the life you dreamed about having. There are few other career choices available that can offer this kind of opportunity.

Impact – Many people want to help their employers or company be successful, but few can make such an impact. When you are running your own business, everything you do will directly impact the company, which can be very rewarding.

Freedom - This is easily the answer most people will give you if asked why they want to become entrepreneurs. Being able to do what they want and when they want to is the driving reason behind taking the risk of running their own business. It is true, having freedom in life and career does make a huge difference!

Responsibility - When running your own business, you can run it the way you feel it should be run. This is especially true if you have the wish to help other people. When you work for someone else, you may not have the ability to help the world the way you would like to, but if you are the boss, you can.

Be your Own Boss - This is another big reason people have for becoming entrepreneurs. When you are the boss, you can do things your way. You can decide your own fate by making your own decisions or taking your own risks.

Time and Family – When you have created a self-sustaining company, being an entrepreneur could give you freedom and time, allowing you to spend more of it with your family. It could also allow you to make your family a part of your company, something you can't do working for someone else.

Create a Legacy - If the idea of creating a lasting legacy is important to you, very few careers allow you to do so, like operating your own business. Just imagine if you were to start a company that could impact millions of people's lives and do it for generations to come.

Accomplishment - If there are specific goals you would like to accomplish in your life, running your own business could help you get there.

Control - For many business owners, the sense of security that comes with controlling your work or destiny is a primary reason to become an entrepreneur.

Now that we covered why you should become an entrepreneur, let's look at what it takes to become an entrepreneur.

Chapter 1 Questions

1 – What are the five reasons that you would like to become an entrepreneur?

2 – Are there any reasons that you would be afraid to become an entrepreneur?

3 – What is the number one reason you would like to become an entrepreneur, and why?

CHAPTER 2: WHAT DOES IT TAKE TO BECOME AN ENTREPRENEUR

"One hour per day of study in your chosen field is all it takes. One hour per day of study will put you at the top of your field within three years. Within five years, you'll be a national authority. In seven years, you can be one of the best people in the world at what you do."

- EARL NIGHTINGALE

T here are plenty of benefits to becoming an entrepreneur, but it is certainly not an easy task to start your own business. Successful entrepreneurs who can accomplish their dreams and goals, earn a living with their businesses, and enjoy the many benefits of entrepreneurship, have specific traits.

If you consider taking the leap and following your entrepreneurship dreams, you will want to understand what these traits are to instill the same characteristics in yourself. This will help ensure that you can achieve your goals.

Successful Entrepreneurs

- Have a lot of passion
- Can manage their fears
- Are tenacious
- Believe in themselves
- Have a grand vision
- Are extremely flexible
- Can defy conventional wisdom
- Are willing to take risks in life

If you have these traits or teach yourself how to develop these traits within yourself, your chances of becoming a successful entrepreneur will increase. In addition to these key personality traits, all successful entrepreneurs possess a certain number of skills.

These Are Some Skills That Will Help You To Become A Successful Entrepreneur

Focus – When running your own business, you will be dealing with any number of factors on any given day. Successful business owners can pinpoint their focus on accomplishing specific tasks and goals at certain times.

Resilience - It is a skill to weather the various ups and downs of business without allowing them to destroy your focus. The truly successful entrepreneurs can travel down the path of success despite what the future looks like.

Management Skills - A successful company needs the right people in the right places, and successful business owners need to know how to manage these people properly.

Long Term Vision - While it's easy to look short-term to see what needs to be done, an exceptional entrepreneur (the ones who see real success in their business ventures) can plan years ahead of time.

Salesmanship - Regardless of what type of company you are running, you need to sell your vision to others to become successful. Truly successful entrepreneurs need to have excellent salesmanship skills whether they want to or not.

Self-reliance - This is one of the most important skills any entrepreneur can have. A business owner must trust that they can depend on themselves.

Self-reflection - The ability to stop, reflect, and learn is a special skill for the entrepreneur. They must be able to learn from their mistakes and reflect on what they've learned in life.

Learning - The skill of learning new knowledge is one that every successful entrepreneur has. It is also a skill they never stop nurturing.

To attain success in your entrepreneurial goals, you must be able to learn from others. The best way to learn a successful business owner's skill is to study the skills of successful entrepreneurs and then develop those skills in yourself.

Chapter 2 Questions

1 – What are the four entrepreneur traits that you currently have?

2 – What are the four traits you need the most help with to become an entrepreneur?

3 – Are there any traits you would like to learn more about?

CHAPTER 3: WHAT IS THE IMPORTANCE OF HAVING PASSION

"If you are working on something that you really care about, you don't have to be pushed. The vision pulls you."

- STEVE JOBS

P assion represents one of the essential parts of becoming a successful entrepreneur. Without passion, running your business would turn out to be just another job. Just think of the most famous and successful entrepreneurs and the kind of passion they had. Here are a few to get you going; Steve Jobs, Elon Musk, Thomas Edison, and many more!

Tip #1 – You should always choose something that you

are passionate about!

Your business dreams will become lost without a lot of passion when you are in the day-to-day grind of running a business. Take a look at the top ten most successful entrepreneurs, and you will see that their passion is the number one driving force behind their success. There is no way to escape this fact - you simply must be passionate to achieve your goals!

Starting With A Dream

The best way to start a business is to take what you are passionate about and find a way to turn that into a business. You need to start with a dream. If you don't have passion for your work, you won't have the motivation and energy to keep pushing through obstacles, you won't be willing to take the necessary risks required to succeed, and you won't be able to sell your dream to others.

Tip #2 – Start with your dreams, and you can grow your business from there.

The unfortunate reality is that once a business reaches the beginning of its third year, its chances of surviving drop dramatically. Only about 44% of companies survive to see their fourth year. Without the passion you get from living your dream, you won't have what it takes to survive year after year. This means that you should start your business from the ground up using your dream as a foundation.

Whatever your dream in life may be, you need to find a way to turn that dream into a business. If your business's foundation is something that you are genuinely passionate about, it will be much easier to grow that dream into a very successful business.

Tip #3 – Don't be afraid to let your dreams and passion change.

Think about all the times growing up and how many times your dreams change. As you grow older and have new experiences, you always see passions change. You might have started with the goal of becoming a pro baseball player, and then it was to become a pro football player, then an astronaut, a doctor, and so on.

The point is that your dreams change and develop over time because your passion is something that can evolve. If what you are currently passionate about isn't something you think you can develop into a successful business, you can learn to become passionate about something different. So, don't be afraid to try new things or ideas; you never know where it might take you.

Chapter 3 Questions

1 – Why should you choose something you are passionate about?

2 – Do you remember how many companies survive to see their fourth year?

3 – Why shouldn't you be afraid to let your passions change?

CHAPTER 4: WHY YOU SHOULD START YOUR DREAM BUSINESS

"All our dreams can come true if we have the courage to pursue them."

- WALT DISNEY

Once you've determined that you have the necessary traits, skills, and passion for becoming an entrepreneur, the next step will be to start your dream business.

How To Get Started

Getting started with your dream business can be the easiest or the most challenging part of the process. It depends on your specific situation. Some would-be entrepreneurs are raring to get started, while others get bogged down with doubts and procrastination.

If you've read the first two books of our Selling for Kids Book Series, you should have hopefully already launched your first business, and this step should come much easier to you. You should be looking at what you can do to launch your dream business now using your experience from our Selling for Kids business model as a guide.

Tip #4 – Don't make excuses about why you shouldn't start your own business.

Once you have made the critical decision that yes, you want to become an entrepreneur, skip the excuses and start the process. It is better to try and fail than never to have tried.

Tip #5 – Avoid the quicksand trap known as procrastination at all costs.

Putting off the process of starting your business for any reason can lead to getting stuck in the mud. Avoid the trap of procrastination as if your life depends on it because it does.

Tip #6 – Do whatever it takes to motivate yourself to get started right now.

Doubt, fear, worry, and a lack of purpose can end up preventing you from getting your dreams going. Focus on why you want to become an entrepreneur (what's your passion) and use that to motivate yourself into taking those first few steps. The first few steps are the most important ones that you will take.

Tip #7 – You must develop core beliefs and be committed to them.

Now is the time to develop your business's core beliefs. These will help you create the right kind of company, one that matches your passion and always motivates you to move forward. Your business's core beliefs will be a significant building block of it, so make sure that these beliefs are worthy.

Your core beliefs will also determine how you make decisions in the future and which direction the business takes your life.

Making The Shift From Employee To Boss

Running your own business takes leadership. It can be difficult for many new entrepreneurs to make the switch from employee to manager or boss. There are ways that you can prepare yourself for this transition. For people who have built-in leadership skills, this transition may be more comfortable, but anyone with the proper drive and motivation can develop the needed leadership skills.

Tip #8 – You can't grow your business

if you don't learn how to listen.

A good boss knows how to listen to their employees and how to recognize good ideas. For a lot of people, the concept of being a good listener is hard to contemplate. Learning how to listen is probably one of the most challenging aspects of turning yourself into a good boss.

Tip #9 – Unless you invite creative thinking, moving forward might be difficult.

Another trait of being a good boss is inviting others to share their ideas with you. You will want to create an atmosphere where your employees will regularly share their ideas with you. Great ideas drive businesses forward and help the employees feel like a part of the company.

Tip #10 – You can't do everything yourself, and you must learn how to delegate.

Maintaining control of a company can also mean delegating specific responsibilities to others, and good bosses know how to do so successfully.

Tip #11 – Always use downtime to reflect on what's happening.

An employee's responsibility to learn from their mistakes is not as great as the boss's responsibility. It's essential to take the appropriate amount of time to stop, think, and reflect upon what you have learned. Only through reflection can you truly learn from your mistakes and avoid repeating them in the future.

Tip #12 – You should always expect respect.

Bosses must require respect. When making the transition from employee to boss, it's essential to expect respect from your subordinates.

Tip #13 – You need to earn respect first.

While you should expect respect from your employees, it's also vital that you be prepared to earn this respect from them. Earning respect is accomplished through honesty, fairness, and giving respect. Essentially, treat others as you wish to be treated.

Keeping Your Options Open

Starting up a new business requires detailed planning. We mean creating various options for running your business and choosing which of these options is the best choice for your particular business. It's essential to keep your options open throughout the entire startup process and even during your business's day-to-day operations to create a resilient and successful business.

Tip #14 – Always be prepared and run a lot of forecasts.

It's always a good idea to run through a series of forecasts for your business. Run through the various "business as usual" projections, then add in other possible scenarios. These will give you different options to overcome any challenges or obstacles that may come up, especially for a new startup business.

Tip #15 – Gather real market information to be prepared.

Very few businesses end up following their business plans. Plans change all the time. The best way to create a valuable and functional business plan is to make sure that you create it using real market information.

Tip #16 – Understand your market because you can't plan what you don't understand.

Gathering real market information for your business's plan means understanding your business's trends, customers, competitors, and various marketing conditions. You need to collect this information by doing detailed market research. Spend the time now to save time later.

Tip #17 – Be prepared and

always plan for failure too.

Things will not always go well in your business. Keeping your options open means understanding this fact and making plans for dealing with failures in advance. Imagine how much better prepared you will be if you plan for losses in advance.

Tip #18 – Deal with what you can control and let the rest go.

While you are making plans for dealing with failures along the way, make sure that you focus on dealing with the things you can control. Constantly obsessing over what you can't control will get you nowhere.

Tip #19 – Always set your personal and business goals.

Business planning is all about setting up goals and then striving to achieve them. There are two types of thinking when talking about setting goals. Some people believe that you need to set realistic goals. The idea behind this to set up goals for your new business that are achievable so that you are not setting your business up for failure.

There is also a second line of thinking when it comes to setting up goals, unrealistic goals. Unrealistic goals are when you set goals high enough that it keeps you pushing forward. It's the idea that it is better to have a plan for making $1,000,000 and fall short of it than it would be to have a goal of just $10,000 and miss that.

Realistic and unrealistic are just points of view. Imagine if Steve Jobs would have placed "realistic" goals in front of himself. Then we would have never had the iPod, iPhone, or most of what we have from Apple.

So, if you set large and "unrealistic" goals, you just may hit them. You'll need to make a choice.

Tip #20 – Remember your dreams but make a plan for your goals.

Dreams are what you want to accomplish with your business, but goals are how you will achieve things—plan for specific goals as a smaller part of accomplishing your dreams. Think of your goals as your roadmap to achieving your success.

Choosing A Business Role That Fits Your Personality

Obviously, as an entrepreneur, your primary business role will be a boss. But this is not the most practical way to plan what you'll be doing for the company on a day-to-day basis. Odds are your company will be more successful if you can create a niche for yourself within the company that fits your specific personality.

Tip #21 – Determine your strengths and make them your business role.

If you are more confident in one aspect of the business, like selling your ideas to other people, that is probably the best place to put yourself in the company. Always play to your strengths. Avoid being in charge of selling the company's ideas to others if you are a horrible salesperson. You will just need to make sure that you hire someone who can sell the company's beliefs.

Tip #22 – Avoid doing it all because you can't.

Very few successful entrepreneurs do it all themselves. A large part of being a great business creator is sharing the load in the most effective way possible. This is why you must hire competent and useful people.

Bringing In Professionals

Since you can't do everything required to create a successful business by yourself, you will have to bring in others. The people you choose to help you operate your company will go a long way towards determining how successful it will become.

One of the essential tasks for any entrepreneur to master is the art of hiring the right professionals for the job. You simply can't afford to lose time, money, and results by hiring the wrong people.

Tip #23 – View your employees as investments in your business.

Every one of your new employees is an investment in your company. On average, the cost of hiring a bad employee for a company is between $25,000 to $50,000 a year. Add in the expense of training and the time for finding new employees, and you can see just how important it is to ensure that you get the proper return on your employee investments.

Tip #24 – You need to hire slow but fire fast.

It's essential to take your time and do the right research when hiring a new employee. Doing it this way helps to ensure that you hire the right person for the job. But be ready to get rid of that person as quickly as possible if they aren't working out. Remember that employees are investments, and you want to drop bad investments as soon as possible. The wrong hire can damage the company's culture and people's morale more than just about anything else.

Tip #25 – Look for competency in all your hires.

Valuable employees have to be competent people. They have the skills, education, and experience to get the job done. Figure out what skills you need and hire only professionals who can prove they have the competency to perform those skills.

Tip #26 – Check for good employee compatibility.

A good employee doesn't only do their job correctly; they can also fit into your work environment. You will want to find professionals compatible with your business, its goals, and its ethics. You also want to hire people who will get along with your employees and customers.

Tip #27 – You must gauge everyone's commitment to the dream.

Turning a startup into a successful business requires tons of commitment from both you and your employees. The right employee is serious about helping the company succeed and commits to seeing it all the way through. One way to gauge a potential employee's commitment level is to look through their work history.

Tip #28 – Look for and choose capable people.

When looking for a new employee, you will want to determine if they can perform their tasks and be likely to go beyond their required duties. A capable employee should grow with the company and take on new responsibilities as they become necessary.

Tip #29 – Choose people that fit into your company's culture.

Tip #29 ties in with Tip #26. Every company has its own distinct culture, including how people communicate with one another, the different expectations regarding their daily work, and the company's various policies.

Employees that don't fit into this culture can often cause problems and diminish efficiency. Therefore, it is always a good idea to hire people that fit well into your company's culture.

Tip #30 – You must plan to compensate appropriately.

It is vital for an employee to feel appreciated and appropriately compensated. If they feel like they are underpaid, they will probably underperform at their job. Plan to pay new employees according to what they are worth and ensure that they are truly satisfied with what you are willing to offer them. Don't be afraid to offer bonuses or commission pay for work well done.

Tip #31 – Speak with former managers and co-workers every time.

Every candidate will provide you with references, but odds are these references are going to give only positive answers to your questions. You may have to dig a little deeper to discover the real facts about a potential employee. Therefore, it is always good to speak with the candidate's former co-workers, including their past bosses.

You will want to make sure any of your questions are also legal to ask where you will be operating your business.

Chapter 4 Questions

1 – What happens when you make excuses about starting a business?

2 – Why should you always run a lot of forecasts?

3 – What's the purpose of hire slow but fire fast?

CHAPTER 5: LEARN TO MANAGE A TEAM OF EXPERTS

"Leadership Is The Ability To Get Extraordinary Achievement From Ordinary People"

- BRIAN TRACY

How well you can manage other people will determine whether your business is successful, and it includes hiring the right employees and finding the right place for you and them in the company's structure. You must choose people who are competent and capable at their jobs. Plus, you must find people who are compatible and committed to your company's culture. By doing this, you will ensure that the day-to-day operations of your company are taken care of.

Preparing yourself for the challenges of becoming a manager will help make sure that you can lead the company to success. But truly successful entrepreneurs don't rely solely on their skills and characteristics. Instead, they surround themselves with experts.

Surround Yourself With Experts

Experts are people who know more about specific parts of the business than you do. It makes no sense to manage every aspect of the business yourself, as it would be to claim that you are the best person to do so. The best thing you can do is to surround yourself with a team of experts to help ensure that the vast majority of the management decisions made are correct and positive.

Tip #32 – Free up your time and make great decisions by hiring experts.

Every decision your company's management team makes will take time and effort to create. You and your team will need to carefully consider the consequences of how a particular decision will affect your company and its bottom line. The more you rely on experts to help you with this research, the more time you will have to run the other parts of your company.

Tip #33 – Always choose niche-specific experts when hiring.

The purpose of hiring experts is to do what's called "OPK," which stands for Other People's Knowledge. The idea is to use other people's knowledge and skills to accomplish specific tasks better than you could by yourself. Therefore, it makes sense to choose experts in particular niches. For example, one of your managers could be an expert in finances, while another is a marketing genius. This way, you don't have to master either of these things to excel in them.

Tip #34 – Recognize your weaknesses and hire to fill them.

The best way to find the right experts is to understand where you need other people's expertise. To do this means you must have an understanding of where your knowledge is the weakest. Don't be afraid of this or too proud to admit it because it can easily be the difference between success and failure.

Tip #35 – Choose experts who can fulfill your business's overall vision.

You need to find niche-specific experts that share the same passions and visions as you, and the odds are your company will see sustained growth.

Why You Need To Be A Positive Leader

Being a leader is a difficult job; it requires many traits and skills. The most important of these is having a positive attitude. Your attitude will determine how you experience every part of your life, including how your business is running. It will also have a tremendous effect on how you act as a leader and how well you can influence your employees.

Even though maintaining a positive attitude every day can be challenging to do, it is one of the most important traits of being a good leader. It can have many positive effects on your business. Start by practicing the following tips.

Tip #36 – Smile a lot and practice in front of the mirror.

One of the easiest ways to maintain a positive mental attitude daily is to smile frequently. When you smile, it becomes contagious and causes other people to smile, and generally displays a happy and positive attitude that others will emulate.

Tip #37 – Always find good things to say to other people.

People like to hear good things said about them. Paying a compliment to someone or saying something nice can go a long way towards changing their attitude and improving their performance. The more you say nice things to people, the easier it will be to come up with something.

Tip #38 – A positive attitude will increase productivity and doesn't cost a thing.

Happy workers are productive workers. The more comfortable and more adjusted your employees are, the harder they will work, and the more productive your company will be.

Tip #39 – You don't need to be unrealistically happy.

Maintaining a positive attitude every day can be challenging, especially when the struggles and stress of everyday life seem to always get in the way. Your employees will be looking to you during the tough times and act the way you do. If you are positive, happy, and upbeat, they will be too.

However, you don't need to be unrealistically upbeat all of the time, or else you may seem fake to them. Even in the most trying times, a simple change in perception or recognition of something positive can make a world of difference.

Tip #40 – Focus on the things that you can change.

Don't try to change things that are beyond your control. Focus your energy on what you can change and work on how you perceive the things you cannot change.

Tip #41 – Always give credit where credit is due.

One of the best things that an entrepreneur can do to create a positive working environment is to give credit to your employees when it is due. No one can do it all themselves, so it is because of all of the employees' hard work when the company is doing well. When deserved, giving credit will increase worker morale and encourage them to keep up the excellent work.

Tip #42 – Whenever possible, give credit in front of others because it's very motivating.

When you give an employee credit for their hard work, try to say positive things to them in front of other employees and even customers. Doing this will increase the employee's praise and show a positive attitude for other people to see. It also increases the image that you are a positive leader.

Tip #43 – Empower your employees by allowing them to make their own decisions.

You chose to hire your employees because of their various skills and traits. Now is the time to empower them to do their jobs by trusting them to make their own decisions. Believe that they are doing their best to help the company achieve its goals and let them do their job. They are your experts for a reason

Tip #44 – Make sure you don't second-guess your employee's decisions.

Even if a specific decision turns out to be the wrong one, it's never a good idea to second-guess that decision because no one likes that, and it will ruin the trust you have built up with your employees.

Instead of continually scrutinizing your worker's decisions, hear them out. Ask why they made a particular decision under the circumstances and use it as a training opportunity.

Tip #45 – Deal with any problems directly, honestly, and timely.

The best way to deal with any problems with your employees is to be both direct and honest. You don't need to crush their spirits, nor do you have to pad them with compliments or sugar coat it for them. Being straightforward will get you far more respect, and it will help you deal with the problem more effectively.

Tip #46 – Never discipline an employee in front of others.

Sometimes being a boss means that you have to "be the bad guy" and discipline an employee. In addition to being direct and honest with your reprimands, be sure to do them in private. Your employee will respect that, and it will help to keep the office attitude positive.

Tip #47 – Do nice things for your employees because it can go a long way.

Actions speak louder than words. Now and then, show your workers that you do appreciate them by doing something nice for them. Sometimes going the extra mile can make a world of difference. Just something simple, like buying them lunch, can go a long way.

Understanding Where Conflict Comes From

Whenever you create a group of people and have them work together, conflict can happen. Conflict is never a good thing in a professional work environment. It can negatively impact your team's morale and productivity, and therefore, your bottom line.

One of the best things you can do as a leader is to understand where this conflict comes from. Once you know its source, you can go about trying to get rid of it.

Tip #48 – Conflicts aren't always bad but don't let it get out of control.

Conflict is bad for business, but it doesn't necessarily have to be the worst thing in the world. It can challenge how people think and possibly create new ideas. After you settle a conflict between two people, there is an increase in trust and respect.

Tip #49 – Remember that a lack of conflict can represent complacency.

The right amount of workplace conflict means that the company is growing and thinking. A total lack of it can mean complacency. There should be some challenging ideas if your company is going to grow.

Tip #50 – Investigate and identify the underlying cause of conflict.

The best way to identify the underlying cause of conflict in your office is to be direct and honest with your employees. Ask them questions. Be prepared to deal with any problem immediately.

Tip #51 – Focus on the positive aspects of conflict and grow from it.

Do you know those positive things like more trust and respect can come out of resolved conflicts? So Do your best to focus on these potential positives when dealing with your employees and their problems.

Tip #52 – Try to allow employees to settle their problems without your intervention.

It is your job to step in when an employee is mistreating another worker or failing to do their job correctly, but you, as the boss, do not necessarily have to get involved with every employee dispute. In many cases, the best course of action is to allow the employees to settle their problems. Let your workers know that a professional work environment is necessary, and while they don't have to be friends, they do have to be professionals.

Tip #53 – Get to know your

employees to understand where conflict is coming from.

There is a lot to know about your workers. You should spend the time and effort getting to know your employees, including their strengths and weaknesses. Getting to know them will help you to understand the source of most types of conflicts that can arise around them and will give you the answers to solving the problem if one occurs.

You Need Listening Skills

Developing your listening skills is one of the most important things you can do to become a great leader and boss. You need to hear your employees because they are a valuable part of your organization. Not only will taking the time to listen to your employees improve their morale and how they think of you as a boss, but it will also help you better understand what's going on in your business. Listening can also open new doors and ideas, which can increase productivity.

Tip #54 – Always let people finishing talking before you begin to speak.

Doing this is a simple yet effective way to improve your listening skills. Simply let the person finish expressing their views before you intervene and try not to think of objections to their points while they are talking. Don't assume you know what they will say before they say it. Simply listen to what they are saying to you.

Tip #55 – Acknowledge the other person's points and show them you understand.

You don't have to agree with their points, but you should at least acknowledge that you understand them. Repeat the person's main concerns in your own words after they have finished speaking to let them know that you have heard and understood them. By doing this, you can dramatically boost morale with your employees, which we'll talk about next.

Tip #56 – Sometimes, just listening can be enough to help.

In some cases, you may not have to take any action to resolve the person's problem. Sometimes simply listening to their concerns and acknowledging that you understand can be enough. Hearing out an employee can often help them feel empowered and significant, which may fix the problem by itself. Sometimes all they need is an ear to listen to their concerns so that they can feel better.

Tip #57 – Let your employees know that you are always available.

Being a good listener also means making sure that people know that you're accessible. Ensure that your employees know that you are willing to listen to them when necessary and that you are available to do so. If they do come to you, make sure that you are not judging them, let them feel comfortable coming to you.

Tip #58 – Remember that your employees aren't just equipment or tools but are people.

It's always a good idea to remember that your employees are people and that sometimes they will have bad days and problems of their own. Of course, it's the employee's responsibility to deal with their issues outside of work, but it never hurts to remember that they are indeed humans. Your employees are not just cogs in your business's wheel - they are the heart and soul of your company, and they deserve to be treated as such, just as you are.

Chapter 5 Questions

1 – Why do you need to hire a team of experts?

2 – What are some ways you can be a positive leader?

3 – Why are listening skills so essential?

CHAPTER 6: WAYS TO STAY MOTIVATED

"You must set targets that are 10 times what you think you want and then do 10 times what you think it will take to accomplish those targets. Massive thoughts must be followed by massive actions."

- GRANT CARDONE

A positive attitude and passion are necessary to become a successful entrepreneur and run a successful business over the long term. Your passion and dreams will be your motivation during this process.

However, the daily ups and downs of running a business, along with the occasional misstep, will often diminish your motivation, which can have severe consequences. The odds of your business surviving for years to come will be reduced without proper and long-lasting motivation.

The good news is that you can do plenty of things to help maintain your motivation and motivate your staff.

Having Positive Thoughts

Again, so much of running your own business comes down to positive thoughts. Staying positive and changing how you think about life can help make sure that you stay motivated during difficult times.

Tip #59 – Don't allow your pride to prevent you from seeking out support when it's needed.

Being an entrepreneur can be difficult work. Sometimes it can help to reach out to others, especially if they are also entrepreneurs. Seeking out support from other people who face similar challenges can help you retain your motivation and find new innovative ways to solve your problems. Support from others can also help you have a little fun and remember why you wanted to be an entrepreneur in the first place.

There are plenty of ways you can seek out other entrepreneurs. You can find many entrepreneurs online at places like Facebook, Twitter, YouTube, and Instagram.

Tip #60 – You must believe in your ability to accomplish your dreams.

Whichever way you choose to achieve this, it is essential to replenish your belief in yourself and do it regularly. Some people accomplish this by creating a motivation wall, while others have regular meetings with a mentor or life coach. Even just taking a few minutes each day to tell yourself that you have what it takes to succeed can motivate you to keep going.

Tip #61 – Everyone needs a break sometimes, so get away from work for a while.

Everybody's mind needs a little rest once in a while. It's essential to get away from your business and your entrepreneurial mindset now and then, simply to allow your brain to rest and recuperate. You should take this time to engage in a hobby and get some exercise in. Exercise is vital to a healthy mind, and by taking some time to relax and refresh, you will find that you can return to work with even more motivation.

Learning How To Manage Your Time

Learning to manage your time correctly will help you be more productive and help ensure that you stay motivated. Every successful entrepreneur has good time management skills. Time management skills can be developed over time and are usually not naturally occurring.

Tip #62 – Forget "clock time".

Traditional time management wisdom helps you manage your "clock time" or actual minutes "on the clock." Clock time is not really how you spend your day. You may want to consider forgetting about "clock time" and think about real-time. Real-time is how much of your day you spend on each activity, both at work and at home. Real-time is relative.

Tip #63 – Choose how much time you should spend on certain things.

Since real-time is relative, you have the power to choose how much of your time you spend on certain activities or tasks. As a business owner, you won't stop all interruptions and problems, but you can decide how much time you want to allocate to dealing with them. Decide how much time you want to spend thinking about things, conversing about things, acting on things, and matching your available time appropriately.

Work When You Are Most Productive

A large part of learning how to manage your time better means learning to organize your work efforts when you are most likely to be the most productive. Working when you are most productive helps eliminate wasted time.

Tip #64 – Record all your activities for a week.

To learn how to work when you are the most productive, you can begin by carrying a schedule book or planner with you and recording all of your thoughts, conversations, and actions for one week. Doing this will give you a better understanding of how much time you spend on each activity, allowing you to determine which activities are productive and less than productive.

Tip #65 – Create a schedule for only the most productive tasks or activities.

Once you understand which activities are most productive and which ones are wasting your time, you can go about ensuring that you only schedule your time around the most productive activities. Schedule blocks of time for yourself for high-priority activities and make sure that you determine how much time is appropriate to spend on each activity.

Tip #66 – You need to have the discipline to ensure success.

Once you understand where and when you are spending your time and if it's on productive or unproductive tasks, have enough discipline to appropriately schedule your time. Discipline is an essential trait that you must develop to ensure your success.

Tip #67 – Every morning, you must take time to plan your day out.

Take about 30 minutes at the beginning of each day to create detailed plans of what you want to do and what you plan to accomplish. Make sure to plan out at least 50% of your day towards your most productive activities or tasks. Also, prepare for times when you will be interrupted. Decide what you want to accomplish before every phone call or meeting to make each more productive.

Tip #68 – Don't be afraid to hang the "do not disturb" sign sometimes.

There will probably be an inevitable part of your day where you need to get work done, and a "do not disturb" sign can help make sure that you can get it done.

Tip #69 – Keep focused, and don't let yourself get distracted.

Your cell phone, social media, and email are great ways to communicate with employees and customers, but they are also incredibly distracting. Plan some time to answer your emails, texts, and calls, but avoid answering a text or call just because it's coming in. Constantly communicating is a drain of your valuable time. You need to understand when a text or call is critical to the business or not.

Tip #70 – There are times when your plate will be full, and not everything will get done.

It's simply impossible to get everything you want to complete in a day. You will never get it all done, and you will drive yourself crazy if you try to do so. These times are where the 80/20 Rule applies. It means that about 80% of the results you produce come from 20% of your time. By learning how to work when you are most productive and making the most of that time, you will complete the most critical tasks.

Tips For Maintaining Motivation

You can do other things to ensure that you stay motivated to keep working towards success every day.

Tip #71 – Don't be afraid to alter your routine.

Routines are often a depressing reminder of the daily grind. By changing it up, even just a little bit, you might be able to create a fresh new feeling. You could do this by having a meeting outdoors or in a coffee shop. Anything that represents something different from your everyday life can have a very refreshing effect on you and your employees.

Tip #72 – Stay in action and keep moving around.

This one may sound simple, and that's because it is. By walking or moving around often, it can help break up the day and keep you motivated. It's also better for your physical and mental health to move around every 30 minutes or so.

Tip #73 – Don't be afraid to

reward excellent work and offer incentives for productivity.

We mentioned this with the compensation tips earlier, but it's so important we feel it deserves its own dedicated one. Offering incentives for yourself and your employees in exchange for hitting specific goals helps with motivation. Incentives are a great way to keep everyone focused on the company and its goals. These incentives don't even have to be related to money. They can be fun things like lunches, prizes, promotions, and even trips. Even the smallest incentive can have a significant effect.

Tip #74 – Keep learning more about your market.

Continually expand your knowledge about your business's market and keep up with the business's most recent trends to help generate new ideas and concepts, which will keep you motivated to grow your company. Doing this will help keep your business always moving in the right direction and better understand what your customers are looking for.

Tip #75 – If you miss it today, there is always tomorrow.

As an entrepreneur, there are going to be days when you don't get it right. It's important to remember that there is always tomorrow. Think of tomorrow as a time to get it right and have massive success. So, if today doesn't go well, there is still the chance that tomorrow will be amazing.

Tip #76 – Enjoy your successes and try to have some fun.

To make your everyday life more enjoyable and more comfortable to deal with, try adding a little bit of fun to your tasks.

Tip #77 – To keep the momentum going, treat the motivation process like a daily task.

You need to complete some tasks every day and week so that your business can remain open. These tasks include the process of motivating yourself and your employees, so make sure that you treat it as such. Finding new ways to stay motivated is essential to keeping your company operational. Make this vital process a part of your everyday tasks.

Chapter 6 Questions

1 – Why should you forget about clock time?

2 – Why is it so important to take at least 30 minutes to plan out your day?

3 – Why are incentives essential to have?

CHAPTER 7: HOW TO KEEP GROWING YOUR BUSINESS

"I think goals should never be easy. They should force you to work, even if they are uncomfortable at the time."

- MICHAEL PHELPS

I f your business isn't growing, then it's failing. If you aren't moving forward, then you're moving backward. After you have the right people in place, your company needs to focus on customers and growth.

There are many ways to encourage growth in your company, and the specifics depend on your particular business. For example, it may mean opening up a new storefront in a retail business, launching an online store, or even developing a new product line. Growth for an IT company could be purchasing or creating a new system.

Whatever your company does, you need to figure out ways to expand it. And this goes well beyond just figuring out ways to earn more money.

Creating Strong Business Relationships

Creating strong business relationships is the foundation of growing your business. Customers, clients, suppliers, and business associates are the lifeblood of your business's future. You simply can't forge ahead on the path to success without these helpers, which means you need to develop long-lasting and meaningful relationships based on trust and honesty with each of them.

Tip #78 – To continue growing, you must communicate often.

Communication with your business contacts is crucial and is especially true of your customers and suppliers. These contacts rely on you to tell them what's going on, including letting them know of any problems you are experiencing. Communication should be a top priority for all your business relationships.

Tip #79 – Never miss a deadline.

When a customer deals with your business, they expect you to hold up your end of the bargain and deliver on what you promised, and this certainly means meeting your deadlines. When you promise something to a customer or supplier, you want them to consider your word as your bond. Customers not having to worry if your business will fulfill its commitments builds trust with them.

Tip #80 – Be prepared and try to prevent surprises from happening.

Customers and clients don't usually like surprises, especially if your company's service directly relates to their livelihood. While it may not be possible for you to prevent all unwanted surprises from happening, being honest with your customers, and maintaining communication with them regarding what's going on can help you eliminate unwanted surprises.

Being Honest With Everyone

We can't state the value of being an honest business enough. Your company will grow much faster and reach further with ethical principles. It's essential to strive for honesty at all times and at all levels of your business.

Tip #81 – Honesty will keep your customers coming back every time.

No business relationship can last if honesty isn't at its core. Being honest with your customers and clients will help them want to continue to give you their business. Honesty builds trust, and this can create a business reputation that will help you grow and get you more clients for years to come.

You should be honest with everyone that has something to do with your business, not just your customers and clients. You need to be honest with your employees, suppliers, investors, and everyone else. You can not make up lies to cover your issues, own up to your own mistakes, and acknowledge the business's state to your employees and investors. Again, this level of honesty creates loyalty.

Tip #82 – To be honest with others, you must first be honest with yourself.

Don't forget that you must be honest with yourself too. It can be one of the hardest things you will ever do. Being honest with yourself regarding what you want from your business and what goals you are looking to achieve is critical. Lying to yourself, even in the tiniest of ways, can end up causing you to compromise your business, ethics, and principles, which can spell disaster for you and your company.

Tip #83 – Be honest about growth and don't lose focus on what's important.

Don't try to grow your business too quickly. There is always the idea that a company should grow as soon as possible, but this idea can often lead to trouble. Sustained business growth comes from a clear and detailed strategy. It also comes from having the appropriate systems and processes ready to cope with this new growth.

Don't focus on everything at one time. Pay attention to the required resources needed to sustain this growth, as many smaller businesses simply don't have access to the right resources and can get in over their heads. Essentially take it one step at a time.

Chapter 7 Questions

1 – Why is it essential to create strong business relationships?

2 – What happens when you are honest with customers?

3 – What can happen if you miss a deadline?

CHAPTER 8:
YOUR SKILLS AT COMMUNICATING ARE THE KEY

"Develop an 'attitude of gratitude.' Say thank you to everyone you meet for everything they do for you."

- BRIAN TRACY

A s you already know, communicating is critical to your business's growth and your company's ability to continue its growth. Communication is also essential for developing trust with your business associates and with your employees.

Good communication skills can motivate employees, drive change, fix conflicts, and help you become a better leader. Listening skills are essential for accomplishing these tasks, but there are other communication skills that all great entrepreneurs need to have.

Better Ways To Communicate

While you are probably good at communicating with other people, there are better ways to communicate when running a business. These are skills you develop over time as a result of your experiences. Learning about some of these skills in advance will help you to incorporate them into your business life as soon as possible.

Tip #84 – Good communication skills will allow you to influence others.

The ability to influence others is vital for any great entrepreneur. You will need to sell your employees your business's principles and goals if you want them to get on board. You will have to convince investors and potential business partners to take a chance and support your entrepreneurial ideas. You will have to influence your customers through marketing and advertising. To get your point across and achieve your goal of influencing others, you must communicate your ideas well through discussions and offer clear explanations of your thinking.

Tip #85 – You are the boss, and you need to learn how to

manage questions well.

As a boss and a leader, you will have to answer thousands of questions. Some of these questions will be simple, while others will determine the success of your company. It's your job to answer them by making convincing arguments using the art of well-versed speaking. Your words must not only answer the question; they must also convey your desires, meaning, and principles simultaneously. If you take the time to learn the art of managing questions well now, it will positively impact your entrepreneurial career forever.

Tip #86 – A great entrepreneur learns how to hold the audience's attention.

You can have the best speaking skills in the world, but it won't help if you can't hold your audience's attention. Learning how to capture your audience's attention is critical, especially in the workplace environment. To master this skill, you must learn how to read your audience, project your voice in a pleasing and attention-getting way, and manage your speaking time. If you can't get people to pay attention to you, it will be hard to get them to follow you to success.

How To Create Dialog

In addition to using your communication skills to motivate and convince others, you can also use them to generate new ideas, incentives, and concepts and use them to your benefit. The best way to do this is to create a dialog. This dialog can be between your managers, employees, customers, and even your competitors. Learning how to start a dialog is another great communication skill that all entrepreneurs must-have.

Tip #87 – For best results, hold face to face interactions as much as possible.

Getting your employees together for face-to-face interactions is a fantastic way to get a dialog going and get everyone's creative juices flowing. Face to face interactions encourages brainstorming and the sharing of ideas in a way that email, text, and telephone conversations can't.

Tip #88 – Provide ways for your employees to communicate with you.

If you want to encourage dialog between your employees, you must provide a way for them to do so. You need to give all your employees a way to offer their suggestions and ideas.

Tip #89 – Make sure you and your management team are approachable to your employees.

All of the communication methods you provide for your employees will be useless if they feel like they can't approach you or the rest of your management team. Use your communication skills, actions, and positive attitude to show your employees that they can come to you with their ideas and feedback. Your employees will come to you if you let them.

Tip #90 – Act on what you hear from your employees to keep them engaged.

If your employees see that you are willing to put their ideas and suggestions into action, they will be much more likely to share them with you. Also, encouraging a dialog among your workers will help you develop ideas and concepts you may have never thought of before. These breakthrough ideas might have never come to you if you didn't encourage dialog with your employees.

Chapter 8 Questions

1 – What can good communication do?

2 – Why is holding the audience's attention critical for an entre-preneur?

3 – What do we mean by creating a dialog?

CHAPTER 9: BECOME A MARKETING GENIUS

"If people like you, they will listen to you, but if they trust you, they'll do business with you."

- ZIG ZIGLAR

A s an entrepreneur, you will need to master many skills, including management, communication, and decision-making. However, one of the most important aspects that all business owners need to understand is marketing. Marketing is how you sell your business to its customers, and therefore it will also represent how you will create profits for your business. There is a lot to understand about marketing and plenty of ways to make mistakes. All successful entrepreneurs have mastered the art of marketing themselves and their company.

Creating A Marketing Plan

Companies that are the most successful in marketing themselves start the process by creating a detailed marketing plan. The size and scope of your business's marketing plan will be determined by several factors, some of which include the size of your company and how many potential customers you will attempt to reach. It's a good idea to create your marketing plan and then refer back to it monthly to ensure that you are still on track. A lot of things can change for a business as the year progresses.

Tip #91 – When you're first starting, your business's marketing plan should cover one year.

The recommended amount of time to plan for marketing, especially if you run a small business or a startup business, is one year. There are a lot of things to cover in a year. Your business will gain and lose employees, the market will evolve, and your customer base will hopefully grow larger. Once your business develops and grows, you can switch to a marketing plan covering two to three years in advance.

The process of creating your marketing plan will be the most challenging part, especially your first time. However, implementing it will be easier than creating it. Expect the process of developing a marketing plan to take up to several months. To make the plan, you should be using your team of hired experts, including people from your finance, supply, management, and personnel departments. Don't forget to hire a marketing expert or experts to help. Make sure to include all your experts' input to make sure that you are not missing anything.

Your marketing plan will have several benefits for your company, including:

Giving your employees something to rally behind – The marketing plan is a roadmap for your employees to see what direction the company is going, what it's going to accomplish, and how it will achieve these things. The marketing plan can give every employee a sense of teamwork and purpose to rally behind.

Providing a set of instructions to follow – A marketing plan is just like a set of instructions. It forecasts a step-by-step plan of how the company plans to succeed, which gives your employees something to follow.

Allows new employees to jump on board quickly – As your company grows and changes, it will take on new employees. The business's marketing plan will clearly define its goals and achievements, which will help new employees jump on board and contribute much faster.

Types Of Marketing Campaigns

There are many different marketing campaigns, and how you decide to market your business will depend heavily on your specific factors. There are several types of marketing campaigns to consider, and you may choose to implement several of these campaign types at the same time or possibly overlapping times. Some of the different kinds of marketing include:

Print advertising – This includes advertising techniques such as magazines, newspapers, and flyers. These allow you to get your brand or advertising information out to specific readers and these marketing efforts usually need to be created months in advance.

TV and Radio – Television and radio ads are great to reach a massive number of potential customers at any given time. These are effective but expensive forms of marketing.

Direct mail – These campaigns focus on brochures, postcards, and flyers sent to customers through traditional mail. This technique is somewhat outdated but still serves a purpose.

Online marketing – This form of marketing would probably be the most cost-effective and most useful marketing type in today's world. These campaigns are usually very targeted and can encompass websites, email marketing, SEO or organic search engine marketing, and social media marketing.

Your marketing team will have to consider several factors for your company's marketing plan. Some of these include your product or service, the person you are trying to reach, what message you are trying to send, and how much money you can spend on marketing.

Tip #92 – Do your marketing research to make sure your priorities are correct.

Research into your market will be the backbone of creating your marketing plan and how you improve it. A lack of good market research will cause you to lose potential customers and sales. There are many ways to conduct market research, including but not limited to, surveys, focus groups, and internet searches.

Tip #93 – You need to determine your target audience ahead of time.

To create an effective way to market to your company's target audience, you must first know who this audience is. Find out as much about your targeted customers as you can so that you can figure out the most effective ways to reach them directly in the future.

Tip #94 – To know what you need, you must clearly define what you have.

You cannot create a detailed marketing plan for your business if you don't know what resources are available for your company. These resources can include how much money you can allocate to marketing and which tactics are available for you. Take the time and see what is there.

Tip #95 – To be truly prepared, make sure your marketing plan is flexible.

Flexibility is an essential trait for every business to have, especially because today's business world is ever-changing, and this is especially true of your marketing plan. Markets and customers continuously change, and your company needs to be able to change with them. Make sure your marketing plan takes these changes into account and is always ready to change with the times.

Existing Versus New Customers

One of your most important jobs as a new entrepreneur will be to find new customers through your marketing plan to help your business grow. Once your business is fully developed, you will continue this journey. Companies that are growing spend a great deal of their time and resources looking for new clients, and because of this, they will often overlook a critical factor. This factor is the retention of existing clients.

Your current customers are a precious part of your business. They have helped you attain success so far and are worthy of your loyalty. You must not forsake them. The fact is that it will cost your business less money to retain its loyal customers than it does to go out and find new ones. It doesn't mean that you shouldn't be spending resources to get new clientele, but it does mean that part of your marketing plan needs to address keeping the customers you already have. The average company will see an annual growth of 3% if they can keep all existing customers for one more month per year. There are lots of ways to work on keeping your current customers.

Tip #96 – Part of your marketing plan should include customer service.

One of the best ways to keep your current customers is to make sure they feel appreciated and happy with your business. Customer service and customer benefits should be included as part of your marketing plan, especially because they cost far less than marketing to new ones.

Tip #97 – Don't neglect your customers and never assume they will stay.

Most people prefer to give their business to companies they trust and like. If you provide an excellent experience to your customers, chances are they will come back the next time. However, don't assume your customers will automatically return to you unless you actively do something to keep them coming back.

There are lots of reasons why a customer may choose to give their business to someone else. Maybe the other company has a lower price, opened up a closer location, or offers better services. Remember that repeat customers will spend about 33% more money at your business on average than a new customer will.

Tip #98 – To build trust, you must be sincere with your customers.

The relationship you build with your existing customers will go a long way towards determining if they will stay your customers. People are good at telling when a company is acting insincerely. Consider long-term retention of your existing customers a worthy goal, and be very sincere in your efforts. You can do this by developing your current relationships and doing your best to make every transaction and interaction as positive as possible.

Online Strategies

Online marketing strategies represent one of the most cost-effective forms of marketing you can use. There are many forms of online marketing available. Here are some of them: email marketing, search engine optimization techniques, social media marketing, lead generation, online branding, and straight-up online advertising.

While the traditional forms of business advertising such as newspaper and television ads are an effective way to reach potential customers, many people find the businesses they want to use via the internet, making online marketing strategies worth their weight in gold.

Online marketing strategies continuously change because the internet is a continually evolving medium. If you want to run a successful online marketing campaign, you need to stay updated with any of these changes. Remember the idea of surrounding yourself with experts. This marketing method may be one of the best examples of how using an expert's skills can help your business succeed. Consider hiring an expert in the world of online marketing.

Tip #99 – Be honorable and always practice white hat marketing techniques.

There are two kinds of online marketing techniques, white hat techniques, and black hat tactics. White hat marketing techniques are those considered honest tactics; they rely on hard work to accomplish. Black hat tactics are ways to cheat the system. These tactics will use strategies that steal customer information from others, blast potential customers with annoying messages, use never-ending link wheels, and load up their website content with keywords to generate false search engine results.

Major search engines like Google have ways to find people who use black hat tactics and severely punish them. Considering how many people use Google to locate companies, you need to understand this warning and not use these tactics. Also, many black hat tactics will alienate and annoy your customers, so it's best to always stick to white hat marketing.

Tip #100 – SEO is critical, and you must pay attention to SERPs.

SERPs are search engine results pages. These are the pages that come up when a customer searches on major search engines like Google. Research shows that most online viewers will only choose companies and websites listed on the first SERP page they receive. If your business's website or links leading to its website don't appear in the top ten results on a major search engine, then people are not finding you.

The need to gain high SERP rankings has led to the creation of SEO or search engine optimization. There is an entire world of SEO marketing out there, and it's worth your time to make sure that you are optimizing your website for high rankings. SEO can include things like keyword generation, Google Ad Word campaigns, content marketing, social media use, positive link building, and connections with high ranking "authority" websites. These are another example of where an online marketing expert can make a world of difference.

Tip #101 – Use every social media channel to help your business explode in sales.

As I'm sure you realize, social media is huge in today's online world. Your customers are using social media, and you should be too. Social media is an inexpensive way to market your company. For example, you can use various social media platforms to establish your company as an authority in a specific niche, directly connect with your customers, and create a brand image for your business. You can also resolve customer complaints and problems, announce news and updates about your company and improve your customer service. You can get all of this accomplished for virtually no cost, making social media marketing a great choice.

Tip #102 – Get the edge over your competition and use content marketing.

Content marketing is another useful form of online marketing that is both effective and inexpensive. Many companies overlook this form of marketing, which can be a big mistake and give you an edge over the competition. Content marketing can include things like podcasts, eBooks, articles, videos, games, and blogs. You can use content marketing to inspire confidence and knowledge about your company.

60% of consumers report having better feelings about companies after they read a custom publication about them. Just be sure that the content you produce is high quality because low-quality content will make your company look unprofessional in your customers' eyes and will get you penalized by major search engines such as Google.

Chapter 9 Questions

1 – Explain why you should become a marketing genius?

2 – What is the importance of having a marketing plan?

3 – Why is online marketing the best choice for many small businesses?

CHAPTER 10:
CREATING THE
ENTREPRENEUR'S
MINDSET

"Success is not something that happens to you. It's something that happens because of you and because of the actions that you take."

- GRANT CARDONE

There is a significant difference between people who start their own companies and truly successful entrepreneurs. Many people start their businesses, but few people achieve the kind of success they dreamed of initially. What is the difference between people who start up their own business and very successful entrepreneurs? The answer is the entrepreneur's mindset.

Few People Think Like True Entrepreneurs

There is a difference between creating a job for yourself and creating a business. A business is something that could still be operational if you, the founder, was to leave. That means you have made a fully functional entity, not just a job position where you do all of the work. This mindset is the type you must have if you want to become a truly successful entrepreneur.

Creating an entrepreneurial mindset starts at the very beginning before you do anything to start up your business. It means having a grand vision of what you want your company to be before it even exists. It means imprinting your vision, dreams, and principles into the company right from the beginning.

You need to ask yourself meaningful questions so that you can focus on more than just the day-to-day functions of running your company. You must build your business on your ideas, dreams, passions, and your principles. That is the difference between working at a job and starting a business.

Prepare Your Character And Personality To Become An Entrepreneur

In addition to how you view your business, you also need to make sure that your personality and character are ready for the challenges of being an entrepreneur. Becoming a very successful entrepreneur takes a lot of hard work and dedication.

Some of the personality and character traits required to become successful in this lifestyle include detailed organizational skills, the ability to handle lots of pressure, a tolerance for risk, a strong mental drive, a competitive nature, a healthy outlook on life, a positive attitude, decisiveness, patience, optimism, and pure strength. This lifestyle also requires self-confidence and independent thought.

It's possible to develop an entrepreneurial mindset into your daily life if you don't already have it. Some people are just naturally designed to be amazing entrepreneurs, while others have to develop these traits within themselves. It doesn't matter which of these two examples you happen to be. As you have learned, true entrepreneurism comes from desire and passion. If you have the right amount of desire and passion for achieving something, then you will have the needed drive to make all necessary changes to yourself to make these things come true. Welcome to the art of developing an entrepreneur's mindset.

Taking What You Have Learned And Incorporating It Into How You Think

Having an entrepreneur's mindset means incorporating everything you have learned into how you think and act daily. It means to focus your energy on what is needed to succeed in your life, which includes being successful in your business. A successful entrepreneur does what is necessary to do their job right, like learning how to focus on the positive aspects, overcome their faults, and learn as much as possible whenever they can.

A true entrepreneur is never off the clock, even though they know when to work and relax. You can apply the entrepreneur's mindset to every aspect of your life. It's not just how you run your company. If you think like a true entrepreneur, you can use it to improve your relationships with your friends and family, develop your interests and hobbies, and your parenting skills. Entrepreneurs are flexible, competent, and able learners. There is almost nothing in this life that they can't do or accomplish, especially if there is lots of drive and passion behind their motivations.

Living The Entrepreneur Lifestyle

There are plenty of benefits to living the entrepreneur lifestyle. For many entrepreneurs, this lifestyle equals freedom, purpose, and enjoyment. It also means lots of hard work and unlimited motivation. The successful entrepreneur lives for their work. It doesn't mean that their job is the only thing in their life - it means that their work is their life's passion because it's their dream. Can you imagine waking up every day to go to a job you love and can't wait to do? If you choose something you are very passionate about, you can achieve a successful entrepreneur's lifestyle.

The entrepreneur's lifestyle is also one of the main reasons why you will want to undergo this amazing transformation. It's why you want to do something different and more meaningful with your life. It's about having another choice. It's not the "rat race" or the "daily grind." It's not "working for the man." It's working for yourself, by yourself, and for what you appreciate the most in life. It's a life choice.

Enjoying Your Success

Hopefully, you will have what it takes to become a truly successful entrepreneur and will be able to push yourself to accomplish everything that it takes to be successful. If you can achieve these feats, you will be able to experience what few other people in this world will be able to feel - the ability to enjoy your success in life.

Almost all forms of success bring the pleasure and pride of achievement with them, but few will taste as sweet as a self-made success. It's a truly fantastic thing to be able to look at your successful life, which includes your passion, dreams, your ability to live the kind of life you always wanted, and your financial security, and know that it was you who created it! There are so few people who have only themselves to thank for the amazing life they live. This feeling is worth more than any money, or material possessions can provide. It's a feeling that you can only experience through the success of entrepreneurship.

The purpose behind becoming an entrepreneur is to take the time to stop and enjoy your success. If not, what's the point of all of your hard work?

Have You Got What It Takes

So, if you think you have what it takes to take on the challenge and develop an entrepreneurial mindset, you should immediately begin the process of doing just that. The good news is that there are numerous tools available to help you along the way, from mastering the necessary skills and personality traits of successful entrepreneurs and business owners to learning the finer points of marketing your business. There are thousands upon thousands of learning tools out there to help you achieve your goals. If you are willing to learn the knowledge and gain the skills, it will be easy for you to find.

You Need To Consume Knowledge Daily

The best advice anyone can give an aspiring entrepreneur is to take advantage of the information age we live in and to learn as much as you can whenever you can. Smart people take every advantage they can find, and with the vast amounts of information available, it's certainly a considerable advantage.

Develop The Entrepreneur Mindset

Learn what you need to know to become a successful entrepreneur, and then create a mindset within yourself that allows you to make the appropriate changes to your physical and mental self.

There is nothing you can't do if you set your mind to it!

Thank you, and we will see you next time in Selling for Kids Volume 4!

Chapter 10 Questions

1 – What is the difference between someone starting their own business and a truly successful entrepreneur?

2 – What are some reasons you would like to live the entrepreneur lifestyle?

3 – Why should you enjoy your success?

SPECIAL OFFER - FREE EBOOK

We Want You To Get The Most From The Selling For Kids Book Series

Don't Forget to Grab your FREE Bonus eBook from Selling for Kids. This is an exclusive offer for Readers of The Selling for Kids Series. It's currently not available on Amazon and only available from the link below.

SellingForKids.com/BONUS

ABOUT THE AUTHOR

Tanya Rogers

Tanya Rogers is a 17-year-old author, entrepreneur, blogger, content creator, podcaster, and high school senior. Along with her family, Tanya has dedicated her time to creating the Selling for Kids Book Series to inspire and teach future young entrepreneurs how to start their own business.

Her mission for the future is to become a public speaker and CEO of a company that allows businesses to thrive financially with the proper sales training. She hopes to achieve a Double Major in Business Management and Economics.

She's created two blogs for education and finance. She also runs a podcast where she talks about business-related topics and tips to achieve mental health. Plus, she's co-writer with other authors on the Chang'E Project, a non-profit feminist organization dedicated to breaking down gender-based stigmas and improve women's education.

ABOUT THE AUTHOR

David Rogers

David Rogers is an entrepreneur, author, trainer, and public speaker. David has been in sales for almost 30 years and dedicates most of his time to training and teaching.

Along with his daughter, Tanya, and son Ethan, David has dedicated his time to creating the Selling for Kids Book Series to inspire and teach future young entrepreneurs how they can start their own business. Their primary focus has been teaching an easy and inexpensive method for kids and teens to start their first business.

They have recently gone digital and created sellingforkids.com as a virtual resource for future entrepreneurs.

On sellingforkids.com, you will find FREE budgeting and tracking forms, videos, articles, and much more!

Read more on the Web Resources page.

SELLING FOR KIDS
BOOK SERIES

Selling for Kids The Book Series was created to help teach and inspire a future generation of young entrepreneurs.

The Kids Guide To Selling: How I Was Able To Make $4,000 In 60 Days

In our first book, The Kids Guide to Selling, we teach you about the nine fundamental principles you need to know to start your first business. Plus, you learn what you need to do Right Now to start selling and generating an income, following our simple and inexpensive business model.

The Teens Guide To Starting Your Own Business: Your Step By Step Blueprint To Becoming A Teen Entrepreneur

In our second book, The Teens Guide to Starting Your Own Business, we dig even deeper into the concepts of starting your own business and becoming a teen entrepreneur. Plus, we give you the step-by-step Blueprint of what, when, and how you need to do to launch your first business successfully.

WEB RESOURCES

The Selling for Kids Series has recently gone digital and created the SellingForKids.com website as a virtual resource for future young entrepreneurs.

On SellingForKids.com you will find FREE budgeting and tracking forms, videos, articles and much more!

Come by and check it out, SellingForKids.com

Plus, don't forget to get your Free Exclusive eBook at

SellingForKids.com/BONUS

Printed in Great Britain
by Amazon